Copyright © 2011 LoveBook™ LLC
Cover and Internal Design © 2011 LoveBook™ LLC
Cover Design and Illustration by Kim Chapman
Interior Illustrations by Robyn Smith
Revised 3rd Edition

Published by Neuron Publishing
www.neuronpublishing.com
www.LoveBookOnline.com

The LoveBook™
Activity Book
For Couples

About this book:

This activity book is not meant to be for relationship repair or an advice tool. It is simply a fun way to spend some time with your partner, learning a little about each other, and having a great time doing it. However, it can be used to build on your existing relationship, whether you are just dating or have been married for 50 years. Part of a great relationship is learning about one another, sharing your thoughts, and doing fun activities together. What better way to do this than with The Activity Book Meant to be Shared™!

How to use this book:

It is really up to you! You can fill out your entire section, and then have your partner fill out their section. Or you may want to complete one activity at a time, then compare your answers. The only requirement is to have fun while filling it out!

Games For Her To Play

How Well Do You Know Your Significant Other?

How to play: Answer the following questions based on what you think their answer would be. Once you're done, read the Q & A's out loud, and compare answers to see how well you really know them!

1. What color are their eyes? (No peeking!) _____

2. What is their favorite food? _____

3. What is their favorite color? _____

4. List their three best friends: _____

5. How do they get dressed (top to bottom, or bottom to top)? _____

6. What famous person (dead or alive) would they like to have lunch with? _____
_____

7. Where is their dream vacation spot? _____

8. Who is their hero? _____

9. How would they spend one million dollars? _____
_____

10. If they were stranded on a deserted island, what three things would they take?
_____

11. What is their favorite memory the two of you have made together? _____
_____

12. If they could have any superpower, what would it be?
_____
_____

If You Were A...

How to play: Fill in the blanks with what you think your spouse/boyfriend/girlfriend would be. Explaining your answers is the best part!

1. If you were a car, you'd be a _____

2. If you were a superhero, you'd be _____

3. If you were a type of food, you'd be a _____

4. If you were an alcoholic beverage, you'd be a _____

5. If you were a plant, you'd be a _____

6. If you were an animal, you'd be a _____

7. If you were any country, you'd be _____

8. If you were a musical instrument, you'd be a _____

9. If you were a toy, you'd be a _____

10. If you were an article of clothing, you'd be _____

11. If you were a flavor of jellybean, you'd be a _____

12. If you were a color, you'd be _____

13. If you were an appliance, you'd be a _____

14. If you were a sport, you'd be _____

15. If you were a quote, you'd be_____

16. If you were a book, you'd be_____

17. If you were a store, you'd be_____

Dress Me Up!

How to play: On the stick figure, draw the style that you like most on your better half. Include clothing, a hairstyle, and accessories!

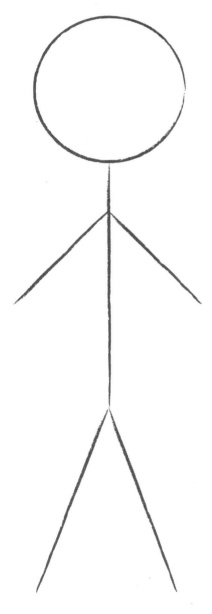

Map Of The World

How to play: Label places you've been together, and places that you'd like to visit in the future!

Rank Traits

How to play: Rank these relationship traits in order of importance to you.
Trade answers with your sweetie to get to know them better!

__ Trustworthiness   __ Respect

__ Honesty   __ Intelligence

__ Sense of Humor   __ Non-Judgemental

__ Sexiness   __ Similar Interests

__ Selflessness   __ Active

__ Caring   __ Responsible

__ Thoughtfulness   __ Supportive

__ Sympathy   __ Confidence

__ Kindness

__ Understanding

__ Appreciative

__ Intimacy

The Matching Game

How to play: Based on what you think of your honey's body, match the body parts on the left with the adjective that best describes them on the right. You can even write in your own "body part" ideas in the blanks!

Back	Sexy
Neck	Hairy
Legs	Cute
Arms	Adorable
Belly	Masculine
Chest	Feminine
Feet	Soft
Hands	Hard
Fingers	Gorgeous
Toes	Beautiful
Hair	Big
Eyes	Small
Butt	Curvy
Ears	Muscular
Mouth	Sweet
Lips	Stunning
Nose	Dainty
_____	Firm
_____	Strong
_____	Handsome
	Pretty
	Graceful

All About Them...

How to play: Write about your favorites memories with your sweetie, things you love about them, etc. Makes a great keepsake!

My favorite time with you:

Songs that remind me of you:

Most adorable thing about you:

Activity I love watching you do:

My favorite thing to do with you:

Our funniest memory:

Our most embarrassing moment together:

Quotes that remind me of you:

ME!

Favorite Body Part

How to play: On the stick figures, circle the body part (or parts) that you find most attractive, sexy, or just adorable on your partner!

Front   Back

Your Favorite Dream

How to play: Draw your favorite/most memorable dream about your sweetie in the dream bubble

Facial Expressions

How to play: Listed under each head is an emotion. Draw the facial expression that your significant other makes when they are experiencing that emotion. Don't enjoy drawing? Paste a photo instead!

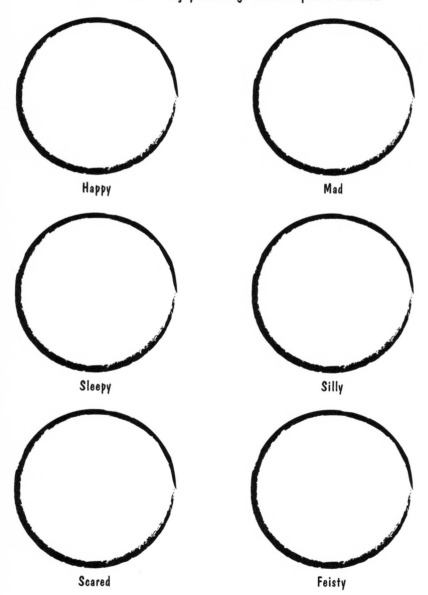

Happy

Mad

Sleepy

Silly

Scared

Feisty

Their Favorite Season

How to play: Draw you and your sweetie into the scene of their favorite season. Recreate a memorable moment you have shared during that time!

13

Their Favorite Holiday

How to play: Pick your significant other's favorite holiday(s). Maybe write a memorable story or funny anecdote to read later and reminisce about!

Christmas	Halloween	Independence Day
New Years	Hanukkah	Mother's Day
Valentine's Day	Rosh Hashanah	Father's Day
St. Patrick's Day	Yom Kippur	Ramadan
Labor Day	Kwanzza	Chinese New Year
Memorial Day	Mardi Gras	Martin Luther King Day
Thanksgiving	April Fool's Day	Passover
Easter	Cinco De Mayo	Purim

_____

_____

_____

_____

_____

_____

_____

_____

_____

_____

_____

Their Favorite Restaurant

How to play: Draw their favorite restaurant, or a memorable moment you have shared during a night out!

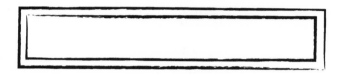

Their Favorite TV Show

How to play: Draw your honey's favorite show or movie on the screen.

Top 10 Adjectives

How to play: Circle the top ten adjectives that you love in your partner.

Gentle

Courageous

Feisty

Trustworthy

Energetic

Sympathetic

Sexy

Calm

Goofy

Outgoing

Kind

Silly

Honest

Sensitive

Cheerful

Loving

Intelligent

Humorous

Likable

Exotic

Appreciative

Creative

Friendly

Passionate

Flexible

Understanding

Good Looking

Adventurous

Responsible

Caring

Selfless

Loyal

Muscular

Grateful

Accommodating

Comfortable

Active

Beautiful

Sincere

Handsome

Thoughtful

Supportive

Intimate

Cooperative

Confident

Sweet

Devoted

Easy-Going

Fun

Non-Judgemental

Romantic

Classy

Respectful

Games For Him To Play

How Well Do You Know Your Significant Other?

My eyes are green

How to play: Answer the following questions based on what you think their answer would be. Once you're done, read the Q & A's out loud, and compare answers to see how well you really know them!

1. What color are their eyes? (No peeking!) _____

2. What is their favorite food? _____

3. What is their favorite color? _____

4. List their three best friends: _____

5. How do they get dressed (top to bottom, or bottom to top)? _____

6. What famous person (dead or alive) would they like to have lunch with? _____
_____

7. Where is their dream vacation spot? _____

8. Who is their hero? _____

9. How would they spend one million dollars? _____
_____

10. If they were stranded on a deserted island, what three things would they take?
_____

11. What is their favorite memory the two of you have made together? _____
_____

Her eyes are hazel!

12. If they could have any superpower, what would it be?
_____
_____

19

If You Were A...

How to play: Fill in the blanks with what you think your spouse/boyfriend/
girlfriend would be. Explaining your answers is the best part!

1. If you were a car, you'd be a _____

2. If you were a superhero, you'd be _____

3. If you were a type of food, you'd be a _____

4. If you were an alcoholic beverage, you'd be a _____

5. If you were a plant, you'd be a _____

6. If you were an animal, you'd be a _____

7. If you were any country, you'd be _____

8. If you were a musical instrument, you'd be a _____

9. If you were a toy, you'd be a _____

10. If you were an article of clothing, you'd be _____

11. If you were a flavor of jellybean, you'd be a _____

12. If you were a color, you'd be _____

13. If you were an appliance, you'd be a _____

14. If you were a sport, you'd be _____

15. If you were a quote, you'd be _____

16. If you were a book, you'd be _____

17. If you were a store, you'd be _____

Sense and
Sensibility

Dress Me Up!

How to play: On the stick figure, draw the style that you like most on your better half. Include clothing, a hairstyle, and accessories!

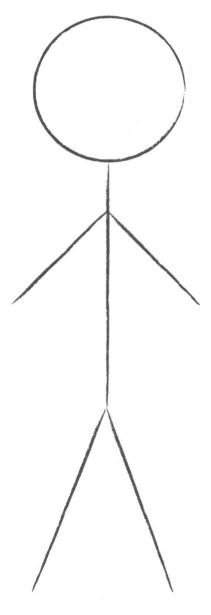

Map Of The World

How to play: Label places you've been together, and places that you'd like to visit in the future!

Rank Traits

How to play: Rank these relationship traits in order of importance to you.
Trade answers with your sweetie to get to know them better!

__ Trustworthiness

__ Honesty

__ Sense of Humor

__ Sexiness

__ Selflessness

__ Caring

__ Thoughtfulness

__ Sympathy

__ Kindness

__ Understanding

__ Appreciative

__ Intimacy

__ Respect

__ Intelligence

__ Non-Judgemental

__ Similar Interests

__ Active

__ Responsible

__ Supportive

__ Confidence

The Matching Game

How to play: Based on what you think of your honey's body, match the body parts on the left with the adjective that best describes them on the right. You can even write in your own "body part" ideas in the blanks!

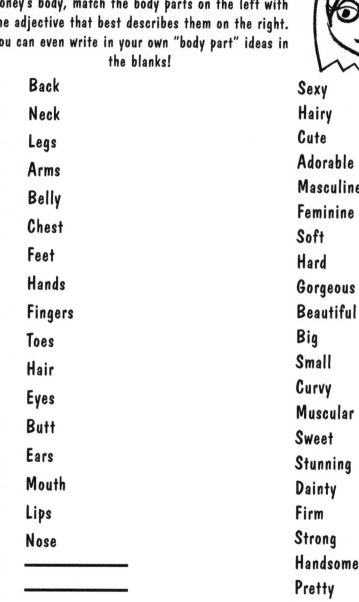

Back	Sexy
Neck	Hairy
Legs	Cute
Arms	Adorable
Belly	Masculine
Chest	Feminine
Feet	Soft
Hands	Hard
Fingers	Gorgeous
Toes	Beautiful
Hair	Big
Eyes	Small
Butt	Curvy
Ears	Muscular
Mouth	Sweet
Lips	Stunning
Nose	Dainty
—————	Firm
—————	Strong
—————	Handsome
	Pretty
	Graceful

All About Them...

How to play: Write about your favorites memories with your sweetie, things you love about them, etc. Makes a great keepsake!

My favorite time with you:

Songs that remind me of you:

Most adorable thing about you:

Activity I love watching you do:

My favorite thing to do with you:

Our funniest memory:

Our most embarassing moment together:

Quotes that remind me of you:

ME!

Favorite Body Part

How to play: On the stick figures, circle the body part (or parts) that you find most attractive, sexy, or just adorable on your partner!

Front   Back

Your Favorite Dream

How to play: Draw your favorite/most memorable dream about your sweetie
in the dream bubble

Facial expressions

How to play: Listed under each head is an emotion. Draw the facial expression that your significant other makes when they are experiencing that emotion. Don't enjoy drawing? Paste a photo instead!

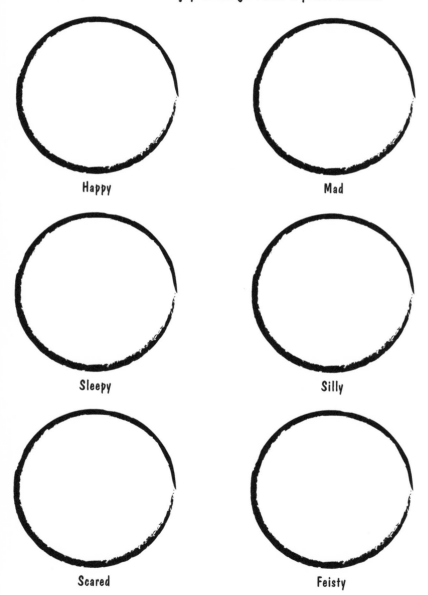

Happy

Mad

Sleepy

Silly

Scared

Feisty

Their Favorite Season

How to play: Draw you and your sweetie into the scene of their favorite season. Recreate a memorable moment you have shared during that time!

Their Favorite Holiday

How to play: Pick your significant other's favorite holiday(s). Maybe write a memorable story or funny anecdote to read later and reminisce about!

Christmas	Halloween	Independence Day
New Years	Hanukkah	Mother's Day
Valentine's Day	Rosh Hashanah	Father's Day
St. Patrick's Day	Yom Kippur	Ramadan
Labor Day	Kwanzza	Chinese New Year
Memorial Day	Mardi Gras	Martin Luther King Day
Thanksgiving	April Fool's Day	Passover
Easter	Cinco De Mayo	Purim

_____

_____

_____

_____

_____

_____

_____

_____

_____

_____

Their Favorite Restaurant

How to play: Draw their favorite restaurant, or a memorable moment you have shared during a night out!

Their Favorite TV Show

How to play: Draw your honey's favorite show or movie on the screen.

Top 10 Adjectives

How to play: Circle the top ten adjectives that you love in your partner.

Gentle
Courageous
Feisty
Trustworthy
Energetic
Sympathetic
Sexy
Goofy
Outgoing
Kind
Silly
Calm
Honest
Sensitive
Cheerful
Loving
Intelligent
Humorous
Likable
Exotic
Appreciative
Creative
Friendly
Passionate
Flexible
Understanding
Good Looking
Adventurous
Responsible
Caring
Selfless
Loyal
Muscular
Grateful
Accommodating
Comfortable
Active
Beautiful
Sincere
Handsome
Thoughtful
Supportive
Intimate
Cooperative
Confident
Devoted
Sweet
Easy-Going
Fun
Non-Judgemental
Romantic
Classy
Respectful

Games To Play Together

Road Trip

How to play: Fill in the blanks to finish the story and create a funny memory with your honey!

One day, I surprised my _____ with a road

term of endearment

trip. With no destination in mind, we _____ into

verb - past tense

the car and _____ away. First, we stopped at a

verb - past tense

_____ for snacks and to fill up with _____.

type of building ___ noun - plural

By _____ O'clock we were on our way! We drove through the

a number

_____ forests and _____ mountains. We held _____ while

adjective ___ adjective ___ body part -plural

listening to our favorite song, _____, on the radio.

name of a song

The scenery was so _____ we pulled out the _____ and took

adjective ___ noun

pictures. On our way home, we found

a _____ restaurant to stop at

adjective

and _____ . After _____

verb ___ a number

_____ we finally made

unit of measure - plural

it home. I would have to say, it was

the most _____ trip we

adjective

had taken together.

35

Romantic Getaway

How to play: Fill in the blanks to finish the story and create a funny memory with your honey!

For our first _____ getaway, we decided to travel
adjective

by _____ to our dream vacation spot in _____. We
noun _a place_

planned for_____ to be sure the vacation was perfect.
unit of time - plural

After traveling for_____ hours, we finally arrived at the
a number

_____ , and immediately checked in. Our room was
type of building

absolutely_____! We decided to head down to the
adjective

_____ to enjoy a_____lunch. As the sun set, we took
noun _adjective_

a relaxing_____on the beach. Holding_____,
verb _body part - plural_

we felt so_____to be alone
an emotion

together. The rest of our vacation was

spent_____and_____.
activity _activity_

After_____of days of relaxation,
a number

we headed home. Overall, it was the

most _____ vacation ever!
adjective

36

Would You Rather...

How to play: Out of the two scenarios, each of you choose which one you'd rather do.

1. Drive the car or ride passenger? 1. _____ 2. _____

2. Lose your sight or your hearing? 1. _____ 2. _____

3. Be drop-dead gorgeous or hilariously funny? 1. _____ 2. _____

4. Be the smartest person in the world or the best-looking person in the world?
   1. _____ 2. _____

5. Be served breakfast in bed or go out to a romantic dinner?
   1. _____ 2. _____

6. Eat an appetizer or a dessert? 1. _____ 2. _____

For these next questions, take turns creating your own scenarios! For example, would you rather "Eat a <u>worm</u>, or drink a glass of <u>vinegar</u>?"

1. Go backstage with_____, or go on tour with _____ ?

2. Meet your favorite_____, or go on a date with_____ ?

3. Spend one day as _____, or one week as_____ ?

4. Watch a 24 hour_____ marathon, or hang with the cast of
   _____ for a day?

PICK A DOOR! ANY DOOR!

1   2

Hangman

How to play: Based on the given theme, create a game of Hangman that your partner needs to complete! Keep track of what letters have been used by crossing them off at the bottom as they are used. Trace the "hangman" as they get letters wrong. Once the man is complete, game over!

Theme: Most memorable vacation spot

Game Play Area

A	B	C	D	E	F	G	H	I	J	K	L	M
N	O	P	Q	R	S	T	U	V	W	X	Y	Z

Hangman

How to play: Based on the given theme, create a game of Hangman that your partner needs to complete! Keep track of what letters have been used by crossing them off at the bottom as they are used. Trace the "hangman" as they get letters wrong. Once the man is complete, game over!

Theme: Funniest family function memory

Game Play Area

A B C D E F G H I J K L M
N O P Q R S T U V W X Y Z

Truth Or Dare

How to play: Pick a truth or a dare - the rule is that once one is selected, it must be completed! Get creative! Make up your own truths and dares as you go along!

Truths

1. If you could live anywhere in the world, where would it be?

2. If you could be someone for a day, who would it be?

3. What's the one job you would love to do?

4. What is your top secret talent?

5. What is your worst secret habit?

6. What is your guilty pleasure Disney movie?

7. Describe the best dream you've had in detail.

Dares

1. Juggle any three objects.

2. Put on your sweetie's underwear and do a dance!

3. Talk like a pirate for the rest of the game.

4. Draw a bunny face on your face with lipstick, without using a mirror!

5. Perform a striptease.

6. Receive a wedgie from your partner.

7. Put an ice cube down your pants until it melts.

Mind Map Of Life

How to play: We've given you starting points in the bubbles; now you can fill in the additions based on what you and your partner want out of life. It's like talking about your future, visually!

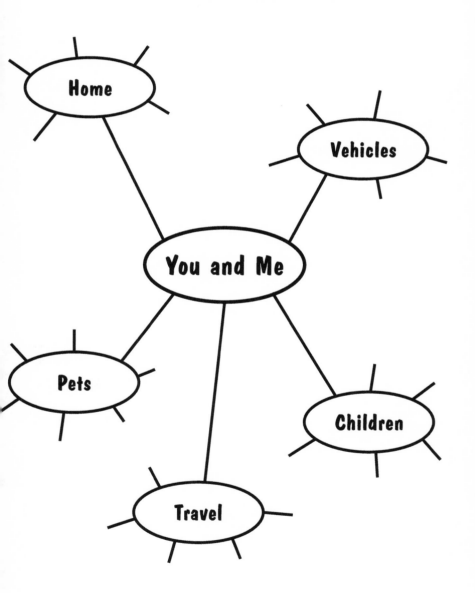

Comic Strip Creators

How to play: Featuring you and your significant other, finish the comic strip below by adding faces and dialogue!

Comic Strip Creators

In the last box, complete the story in your own way!

43

About LoveBook™:

We are a group of individuals who want to spread love in all its forms. We believe love fuels the world and every relationship is important. We hope this book helps build on that belief.